NATURE'S CYCLES

A PLANT'S LIFE CYCLE

A.B. CLAMANT

NORWOOD HOUSE PRESS

Cataloging-in-Publication Data

Names: Clamant, A.B., 1972-.
Title: A plant's life cycle / A.B. Clamant.
Description: Buffalo, NY : Norwood House Press, 2026. | Series: Nature's cycles | Includes glossary and index.
Identifiers: ISBN 9781978575615 (pbk.) | ISBN 9781978575622 (library bound) | ISBN 9781978575639 (ebook)
Subjects: LCSH: Plant life cycles--Juvenile literature.
Classification: LCC QK731.C536 2026 | DDC 571.8'2--dc23

Published in 2026 by
Norwood House Press
2544 Clinton Street
Buffalo, NY 14224

Copyright © 2026 Norwood House Press
Designer: Rhrea Magaro
Editor: Kim Thompson

Photo credits: Cover, p. 1 Romolo Tavani/Shutterstock.com; p. 3 Fahkamram/Shutterstock.com; p. 4 Valentyn Volkov/Shutterstock.com; p. 5 Emvat Mosakovskis/Shutterstock.com; p. 6 sergey kolesnikov/Shutterstock.com; p. 7 alexdov/Shutterstock.com; p. 9 Hayati Kayhan/Shutterstock.com; p. 10 zoyas2222/Shutterstock.com; pp. 10, 11 MEE KO DONG/Shutterstock.com; p. 12 Radu Bercan/Shutterstock.com; p. 13 George Trumpeter/Shutterstock.com; p. 15 LutsenkoLarissa/Shutterstock.com; p. 16 Smeerjewegproducties/Shutterstock.com; p. 17 Iness_la_luz/Shutterstock.com; p. 19 SarahLou Photography/Shutterstock.com; p. 20 Olya Humeniuk/Shutterstock.com

All rights reserved. No part of this book may be reproduced in any form without permission in writing from the publisher, except by a reviewer.

Printed in the United States of America

Some of the images in this book illustrate individuals who are models. The depictions do not imply actual situations or events.

CPSIA compliance information: Batch #CSNHP26: For further information contact Norwood House Press at 1-800-237-9932.

TABLE OF CONTENTS

Where Do Plants Come From? 4

Sensational Seeds 6

A Baby Plant 8

Feeding Itself 12

From Flower to Fruit 14

The Cycle Continues 18

Glossary 22

Thinking Questions 23

Index 24

About the Author 24

Where Do Plants Come From?

Oak trees are tall and leafy. Acorns are small and hard. The two things have nothing to do with each other, right? Wrong! They are both part of the amazing life **cycle** of plants.

Sensational Seeds

All plants begin with seeds. Seeds contain all the information a plant needs to grow. They are protected by a tough outer layer called a seed coat.

Seeds wait for the right conditions before they sprout. Water, soil, and warmth allow a seed to **germinate**. The seed coat splits. A tiny root grows downward.

A Baby Plant

More roots branch out from the first one. The roots search for water in the soil. They hold the **seedling** in place.

A **stem** pokes up through the soil. It keeps growing above the ground. What is left of the seed opens up, forming seed leaves.

The seed leaves feed the little plant until it can make its own food. Once new leaves grow, the seed leaves fall off.

Feeding Itself

More leaves grow upward to trap the sunlight. Small openings on the undersides of leaves are called **stomata**. They trap a gas called **carbon dioxide**.

Using water, sunlight, and carbon dioxide, the plant can make its own food. This is called **photosynthesis**. This amazing process creates **oxygen** too!

From Flower to Fruit

Many adult plants grow flowers. They look and smell pretty. They also contain the parts the plant needs to **reproduce**.

Flowers have male and female parts. The male part makes a powder called **pollen**. It must travel to the female parts. Wind blows pollen. Bees, butterflies, bats, and other animals move pollen too.

When male and female flower parts combine, the flower is pollinated. A pollinated flower can grow into a fruit. Many fruits are good to eat. They also contain a plant's seeds.

The Cycle Continues

Fruits and their seeds drop on the ground.

Seeds blow in the wind or get carried by water.

They get eaten and pooped out by animals.

Then, they wait for the water, soil, and warmth that will let them grow into new plants.

Take a look at a little weed, a garden plant, or a big tree. Think about how it grew. A little seed worked its magic to bring us flowers, fruit, shade, and oxygen!

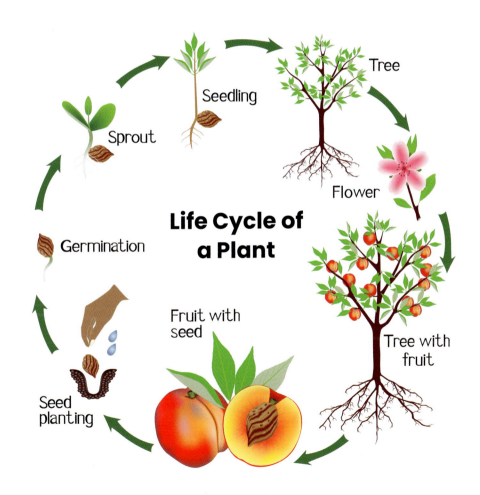

Glossary

carbon dioxide (KAHR-buhn dye-AHK-side): a gas made up of carbon and oxygen that people and animals breathe out and that plants take in

cycle (SYE-kuhl): a series of events that repeat over and over in the same order

germinate (JUR-muh-nate): to put out shoots and begin to grow into a plant from a seed

oxygen (AHK-si-juhn): a gas with no color that people and animals need to breathe in to stay alive

photosynthesis (foh-toh-SIN-thi-sis): the process by which a green plant uses sunlight to change water and carbon dioxide into food

pollen (PAH-luhn): a fine powder made by the male parts of plants to help them reproduce

reproduce (ree-pruh-DOOS): to make more living things of the same kind; to make babies

22

seedling (SEED-ling): a young plant grown from a seed

stem (stem): the main structure of a plant that supports leaves and flowers

stomata (STOH-muh-tuh): small openings on leaves that take in carbon dioxide

Thinking Questions

1. How does the plant life cycle begin?

2. What three things does a seed need to germinate?

3. What three things does a plant need to make its own food?

4. Why are plant roots important?

5. How does pollen move between flower parts?

Index

carbon dioxide 12, 13

flowers 14, 16, 17, 21

fruit 17, 18, 21

photosynthesis 13

pollen 16

roots 7, 8

seeds 6, 7, 10, 17, 18, 21

soil 7, 8, 10, 18

sunlight 12, 13

water 7, 8, 13, 18

About the Author

A.B. Clamant is the author of several fact-filled books for kids. The daughter of two grade school teachers, she developed a love of children's books at an early age. When she's not writing, she is working on opening her own petting zoo, ABCs Animals. Her favorite foods are bread, fruit strips, and candy. A.B. Clamant lives in Springfield, Missouri, with her four cats: Monkey, Corky, Prissy, and Nelly.